Bible Basics
FOR KIDS

TERRY GLASPEY & KATHLEEN KERR

HARVEST HOUSE PUBLISHERS
EUGENE, OREGON

BIBLE BASICS FOR KIDS

Copyright © 2014 by Terry Glaspey and Kathleen Kerr
Published by Harvest House Publishers
Eugene, Oregon 97402
www.harvesthousepublishers.com

Library of Congress Cataloging-in-Publication Data
    Glaspey, Terry W.
    Bible basics for kids / Terry Glaspey and Kathleen Kerr.
       pages cm
    ISBN 978-0-7369-5820-2 (pbk.)
    ISBN 978-0-7369-5821-9 (eBook)
    1. Bible--Miscellanea—Juvenile literature. I. Title.
    BS539.G53 2014
    220.6'1--dc23

                                   2013043554

Printed in the United States of America
      14 15 16 17 18 19 20 21 22 / BP-JH / 10 9 8 7 6 5 4 3 2 1

To Carolyn
As you learn the old, old story

Contents

Before We Get Started

You've got questions.

That's good. Questions are important. Questions like...

Are all these Bible stories true?

Did Jesus really rise from the dead?

Does it actually matter if He did?

Do I believe in God? Or are my parents just telling me I should?

What difference does it make if I'm a Christian or not?

Those aren't questions you can just push to the back of your mind. They're too big. Too important. And the answers just might change your life.

But where do you go to find the answers? The Bible. There's just one problem...

You don't know where to start.

So you flip to a page near the beginning and read, "Do not cook a young goat in its mother's milk." Well...okay. You'll be sure to remember that next time you're cooking a goat. Maybe you'll try a different part. You flip to another page, and this time you read, "The grain offering given with the ram is to be an ephah, and the grain offering with the lambs is to be as much as he pleases, along with a hin of olive oil for each ephah."

Huh?

There's some pretty weird stuff in the Bible. A lot of its stories are strange and hard to understand. After all, it was written thousands of years ago in languages almost no one speaks today. The Bible is a collection of more than 60 books that sometimes seem to say totally different things. It can be confusing!

But if you take a closer look, you'll see that all these stories in all these books come together in one big story, and there's one main character: Jesus. The Bible is the story of God reaching out to His children, showing them over and over again how much He loves and cares for them. The Bible is also the story of how people try to reach back to God...and how they sometimes screw up.

That means it's a story about *you*. You've got a part to play in this story too. God is reaching out to you just like He reached out to Abraham and Moses and Esther and all the other Bible heroes you've heard about.

Think of this book like a tour guide to the Bible. Inside, you'll start to understand how all the pieces of the Bible fit together. You'll figure out how you can read and study it for yourself. And you just might find the answers to some of those questions you've been asking.

Ready? It's time to dig in!

Seven Ways the Bible Helps Us Know and Love God

Look up each verse in your Bible and write it down to help you remember it. What does that verse tell you about God?

1. The Bible helps us look at circumstances through God's eyes. **Romans 8:28:**

   _____

   _____

   _____

2. The Bible shows us the way when we're not sure where to go. **Psalm 119:105:**

   _____

   _____

   _____

3. The Bible helps us find faith in Jesus. **Romans 10:17:**

   _____

   _____

   _____

4. The Bible helps us face temptation. **Psalm 119:11:**

_____

_____

_____

5. The Bible gives us wisdom when we face life's trials.
   2 Timothy 3:16:

_____

_____

_____

6. The Bible is like a mirror, showing us the real
   condition of our hearts. **Hebrews 4:12:**

_____

_____

_____

7. The Bible is like food that helps us grow in our faith.
   1 Peter 2:2:

_____

_____

_____

reading the bible
for yourself

Five Great Reasons
to Read the Bible

Maybe the Bible is brand new to you. You've always thought it was just a really old, long book with tiny print. But you've heard people talk about someone named Jesus and you want to know more about Him. You're just not sure where to start. Is the Bible the best place?

Or maybe you've been hearing Bible stories since practically before you were born. You've heard them in Sunday school and in your family devotions. And you've learned all the songs to go along with them, right? Maybe you've even memorized some verses. You know the Bible from front to back already. So why bother reading it for yourself?

First, because *it contains an amazing message from God.* No other book can claim to be the very Word of God. It's the story of God showing His people just how much He loves them, even when they disobey. That's a message that still matters to us today!

Second, because *it's filled with wisdom about how we should live.* In the pages of the Bible you'll learn how to draw near to God and to other people. The Bible shows us the best way to live.

Third, because *it teaches us about God, about ourselves, and about the world we live in.* The Bible is a mirror in which we learn to see ourselves as God sees us and realize we need to depend on Him.

Fourth, because *you need to meet Jesus for yourself.*

Even if your parents have taught you all about Jesus, you still need to believe in Him and choose to follow Him. That's a decision no one else can make for you. If you're not sure what to think about Jesus, dig into the Bible for yourself to see what He's all about.

Fifth, because _the Bible is an incredible story_. Really! The Bible is full of adventure, romance, war, miracles, anger, forgiveness, and stories that will leave you on the edge of your seat. You'll never be bored when you dig into the Word.

Here's why I want to read my Bible:

1._____

_____

2._____

_____

3._____

_____

Wait—My Bible Says Something Different!

Back in the days of Moses, King David, and Jesus, God gave writers inspired words to record His message. There's just one problem—they wrote that message in Hebrew and Greek! Unless you go to school to study those languages, you'll need to read God's Word in an English translation.

Every language works a little bit differently. Sometimes one word in another language can be translated as many words in English. For example, the Hebrew word *tob* can mean *good, pleasing, high, well done, beautiful, handsome, happy, upright, righteous,* or *pleasant*. Each translator has to choose which word to use, and that makes each translation different.

If you look at the Bibles in a bookstore you'll see that there are lots of different versions. None of them are right or wrong. They just use different words to explain the same idea.

Take a look at how three different Bibles translate a familiar passage—1 Corinthians 13:4-8.

> Charity suffereth long, and is kind; charity envieth not; charity vaunteth not itself, is not puffed up, doth not behave itself unseemly, seeketh not her own, is not easily provoked, thinketh no evil; rejoiceth not in iniquity, but rejoiceth in the truth; beareth all things, believeth all things, hopeth all

things, endureth all things. Charity never faileth **(King James Version)**.

Love is patient, love is kind. It does not envy, it does not boast, it is not proud. It does not dishonor others, it is not self-seeking, it is not easily angered, it keeps no record of wrongs. Love does not delight in evil but rejoices with the truth. It always protects, always trusts, always hopes, always perseveres. Love never fails **(New International Version)**.

Love is patient and kind. Love is not jealous or boastful or proud or rude. It does not demand its own way. It is not irritable, and it keeps no record of being wronged. It does not rejoice about injustice but rejoices whenever the truth wins out. Love never gives up, never loses faith, is always hopeful, and endures through every circumstance...Love will last forever! **(New Living Translation)**.

Is one version harder than the others? Does reading the other versions help you understand it? Circle the passage that's easiest for you to understand.

Four Awesome Tips to Help You Understand What You're Reading

1. **Pay attention to the whole story.** Every verse is surrounded by other verses. To really understand what the author of the book was saying and what God is trying to teach you, it's important to read the entire chapter, passage, or book. It isn't wise to just rip a verse out of context and try to apply it to your life. For example, read 1 Corinthians 13. It's all about *love*. If you read the chapter without looking at the context, you might think it's describing mushy, romantic love. But if you read the chapter right before it, you'll see that love is a spiritual gift we're supposed to share with the entire church body. The chapter is telling us about the kind of love God wants us to show to all Christians.

2. **Ask questions about what you're reading and make sure you are noticing everything the passage has to say.** Whenever you read a story, ask yourself the following questions: Who? What? When? Where? Why? How? Slow down and answer the questions carefully, and you'll be surprised how much more you'll learn.

3. **Don't be afraid to ask for help.** You've got parents, teachers, and pastors for a reason. Talk to them. Learn from them. And start reading! There are lots of great books about the Bible that can give you information you might never discover on your own—the meanings of words, historical background, cultural habits, and how the passages fit into the big story of God coming to earth to save His people. Don't be too proud to ask for help from the experts.

4. **Ask yourself what the Bible means for your life.** You'll miss out if you simply look at the Bible as a dusty old book that doesn't have meaning for you today. As you read, ask yourself how the passage might apply to your life and what you need to do about it. How does God's Word change the way you think and the way you live?

A Bible Highlights Reading Plan

Okay, okay. The Bible's huge. It's got thousands of pages and the print is super tiny. It probably feels like there's no way you'll ever get through it. It would take you a million billion years, right? And where do you even start?

Maybe there's a simpler way to get to know what's in the Bible. You could start by reading some of the highlights—some of the most interesting stuff. You'll be surprised how much you can get out of it if you read just a little bit each day. A few minutes with the Bible will fill your day with wonder, hope, and inspiration.

The reading plan below helps you hit some of the big parts of the Bible. By reading these chapters, you'll see many of the Bible's most famous stories and passages. Mark off each day as you complete your reading. After that, you'll be ready to explore the whole Bible, chapter by chapter. You'll find lots of treasure just waiting to be discovered!

Highlights from Genesis

- ❑ Day 1 – Genesis 1
- ❑ Day 2 – Genesis 2
- ❑ Day 3 – Genesis 3
- ❑ Day 4 – Genesis 6

- ☐ Day 5 – Genesis 7
- ☐ Day 6 – Genesis 8
- ☐ Day 7 – Genesis 12
- ☐ Day 8 – Genesis 32
- ☐ Day 9 – Genesis 37

Something great I learned from Genesis:

_____

_____

_____

Highlights from Joshua

- ☐ Day 1 – Joshua 1
- ☐ Day 2 – Joshua 2
- ☐ Day 3 – Joshua 3

Something great I learned from Joshua:

_____

_____

_____

Highlights from Psalms and Proverbs

- ❑ Day 1 – Psalm 1
- ❑ Day 2 – Psalm 8
- ❑ Day 3 – Psalm 23
- ❑ Day 4 – Psalm 51
- ❑ Day 5 – Psalm 139
- ❑ Day 6 – Proverbs 3
- ❑ Day 7 – Proverbs 6

Something great I learned from Psalms and Proverbs:

_____

_____

_____

Highlights from Matthew

- ❑ Day 1 – Matthew 4
- ❑ Day 2 – Matthew 5
- ❑ Day 3 – Matthew 6
- ❑ Day 4 – Matthew 7
- ❑ Day 5 – Matthew 24
- ❑ Day 6 – Matthew 28

Something great I learned from Matthew:

_____

_____

_____

Highlights from John

- ❑ Day 1 – John 1
- ❑ Day 2 – John 3
- ❑ Day 3 – John 10
- ❑ Day 4 – John 14
- ❑ Day 5 – John 15
- ❑ Day 6 – John 17

Something great I learned from John:

_____

_____

_____

Highlights from Paul's Letters

- ❑ Day 1 – Romans 3
- ❑ Day 2 – Romans 6

- ❑ Day 3 – Romans 8
- ❑ Day 4 – Romans 12
- ❑ Day 5 – 1 Corinthians 13
- ❑ Day 6 – Galatians 5
- ❑ Day 7 – Ephesians 1
- ❑ Day 8 – Ephesians 5
- ❑ Day 9 – Ephesians 6
- ❑ Day 10 – Philippians 2
- ❑ Day 11 – Colossians 2
- ❑ Day 12 – 1 Thessalonians 4
- ❑ Day 13 – 2 Timothy 3

Something great I learned from Paul's letters:

_____

_____

_____

Bible Knock-Knock Jokes

Knock, knock.
Who's there?
Zeke.
Zeke who?
Zeke and you shall find!

Knock, knock.
Who's there?
Hosanna.
Hosanna who?
To wash the car you need a Hosanna tub of soapy water.

Knock, knock.
Who's there?
Luke.
Luke who?
Luke both ways before you cross the street.

Knock, knock.
Who's there?
Eden.
Eden who?
She's Eden up all the snacks!

Knock, knock.
Who's there?
Moses.
Moses who?
He Moses lawn every week.

Knock, knock.
Who's there?
Mary.
Mary who?
Mary Christmas!

Make up your own Bible knock-knock joke and write it here!

_____

_____

_____

_____

_____

Memorizing the Bible

When you go to school, your teacher will often ask you to memorize certain things—dates in history when important stuff happened, the names of the states or state capitals, or the multiplication tables. When you memorize something it means that you know it so well that you can always remember it. You don't have to look it up in a book or ask someone. You just know it. When you need to know what six times six equals, you can say "Thirty-six!" without even stopping to think.

The Bible is God's Word, and it is important to know what God says. You probably won't carry your Bible around everywhere you go, but when you memorize verses you can carry them around in your mind and your heart.

Did you know there is even a Bible verse about memorizing the Bible? It talks about how we can take God's words with us everywhere we go.

> These commandments that I give you today are to be on your hearts. Impress them on your children. Talk about them when you sit at home and when you walk along the road, when you lie down and when you get up (Deuteronomy 6:6-7).

Sometimes you'll feel sad. Sometimes you'll get angry with a friend and feel bad about it. And sometimes a person will ask you a question about God. If you have memorized some Bible verses, you'll remember what God thinks about that situation or be reminded of His love for you. You'll have bite-sized bits of wisdom right at your fingertips!

Amazing Tips for
Memorizing Bible Verses

Learning Bible verses is easy and fun. Here are a few tips for memorizing some favorite verses from God's Word. You might want to try some or all of these little tricks for remembering.

1. *Write it out.* Once you find a verse that you want to memorize, try writing it on a piece of paper or an index card. Writing something down helps you remember it.

2. *Read it aloud,* over and over. Reading aloud also helps you remember. Repeat, repeat, repeat. Once you've said it aloud several times, the verse starts to become permanent in your memory.

3. *Draw a picture* of what the verse means to you or what you see in your mind when you read or hear it. God made our brains in such a way that pictures are easier to remember than just words on a page. Sometimes getting the picture in your mind will give you just the help you need to remember the words.

4. *Share it with a friend* or someone from your family. The best way to keep remembering something is by talking about it. It's like when someone tells you a joke. If you tell it to someone

else, you probably won't forget it. If you don't share the joke, it'll probably slip out of your memory pretty fast. Maybe you can even find a family member or friend who wants to memorize some of the same verses you are working on.

5. **Talk with a parent, pastor, or older friend** about what the verse means. It doesn't do much good just to memorize some words if you don't really know what they mean. Some Bible verses have so much deep meaning that it might take an older person to help you understand them completely. And when you know what they mean, it will be easier to remember them and use them in your life.

6. **Use the Bible verses in your prayers.** When you talk with God, use the words of the Bible to ask for what you need, to apologize for your mistakes and sins, and especially to thank God for the good things He has given you.

Other tips I use to memorize Bible verses:

_____

_____

_____

The first Bible verse I want to memorize is:

_____

_____

_____

Incredible Bible Verses
You Can Memorize

The Bible is filled with so many great verses! Here are some that are especially helpful to memorize. Can you learn them all by heart?

> Your word is a lamp for my feet,
>   a light on my path.
> *(Psalm 119:105)*

Date Memorized: _____

> Trust in the LORD with all your heart,
>   and lean not on your own understanding.
> *(Proverbs 3:5)*

Date Memorized: _____

> But those who hope in the LORD
>   will renew their strength.
> They will soar on wings like eagles;
>   they will run and not grow weary,
>   they will walk and not be faint.
> *(Isaiah 40:31)*

Date Memorized: _____

"Our Father in heaven,
hallowed be your name,
your kingdom come,
your will be done,
    on earth as it is in heaven.
Give us today our daily bread.
And forgive us our debts,
    as we also have forgiven our debtors.
And lead us not into temptation,
    but deliver us from the evil one."
(Matthew 6:9-13)

Date Memorized: _____

"Ask and it will be given to you; seek and you will find; knock and the door will be opened to you" *(Matthew 7:7).*

Date Memorized: _____

"I am with you always, to the very end of the age" *(Matthew 28:20).*

Date Memorized: _____

"Do to others as you would have them do to you" *(Luke 6:31)*.

Date Memorized: _____

For God so loved the world that he gave his one and only Son, that whoever believes in him shall not perish but have eternal life *(John 3:16)*.

Date Memorized: _____

"Do not let your hearts be troubled. You believe in God; believe also in me. My Father's house has many rooms; if that were not so, would I have told you that I am going there to prepare a place for you? And if I go and prepare a place for you, I will come back and take you to be with me that you also may be where I am" *(John 14:1-3)*.

Date Memorized: _____

Jesus answered, "I am the way and the truth and the life. No one comes to the Father except through me" *(John 14:6)*.

Date Memorized: _____

"Peace I leave with you; my peace I give you. I do not give to you as the world gives. Do not let your heart be troubled and do not be afraid" *(John 14:27)*.

Date Memorized: _____

For the wages of sin is death, but the gift of God is eternal life in Christ Jesus our Lord *(Romans 6:23)*.

Date Memorized: _____

And we know that in all things God works for the good of those who love him, who have been called according to his purpose *(Romans 8:28)*.

Date Memorized: _____

For I am convinced that neither death nor life, neither angels nor demons, neither the present nor the future, nor any powers, neither height nor depth, nor anything else in all creation, will be able to separate us from the love of God that is in Christ Jesus our Lord *(Romans 8:38-39)*.

Date Memorized: _____

Love is patient, love is kind. It does not envy, it does not boast, it is not proud. It does not dishonor others, it is not self-seeking, it is not easily angered, it keeps no record of wrongs. Love does not delight in evil but rejoices with the truth. It always protects, always trusts, always hopes, always perseveres *(1 Corinthians 13:4-7)*.

Date Memorized: _____

But the fruit of the Spirit is love, joy, peace, forbearance, kindness, goodness, faithfulness, gentleness and self-control *(Galatians 5:22-23)*.

Date Memorized: _____

I can do all this through him who gives me strength *(Philippians 4:13)*.

Date Memorized: _____

Don't let anyone look down on you because you are young, but set an example for the believers in speech, in conduct, in love, in faith and in purity *(1 Timothy 4:12)*.

Date Memorized: _____

"Never will I leave you; never will I forsake you" *(Hebrews 13:5)*.

Date Memorized: _____

Dear friends, let us love one another, for love comes from God. Everyone who loves has been born of God and knows God. Whoever does not love does not know God, because God is love *(1 John 4:7-8)*.

Date Memorized: _____

Ridiculous Bible Riddles

(See the answers on the next page)

1. Why was Moses the most sinful man in the whole Bible?

2. What two things do John the Baptist and Winnie the Pooh have in common?

3. Is the book of Hezekiah in the Old Testament or the New Testament?

4. Why was Moses buried in the land of Moab?

5. What two things did Samson never eat for breakfast?

6. Where is baseball mentioned in the Bible?

7. Where is tennis mentioned in the Bible?

8. What kind of man was Boaz before he got married?

9. How do we know the apostles had an automobile?

10. What man in the Bible had no parents?

Answers to
Ridiculous Bible Riddles

1. He broke all ten commandments at once (Exodus 32:19).

2. They both eat honey and have the same middle name.

3. Neither. There is no such book in the Bible.

4. Because he was dead.

5. Lunch and dinner.

6. Genesis 1:1—"In the big inning..."

7. When Joseph served in Pharaoh's court (Genesis 39–47).

8. Ruth-less (see the book of Ruth).

9. Because the Bible says they were "all in one Accord" (Acts 1:14).

10. Joshua the son of Nun (Exodus 33:11).

Part 2

a TOUR OF THE BIBLE

A Quick Look at the Entire Bible

The events of the Bible took place over thousands of years, but the stories can be grouped into a few different time periods to help you understand the story of how God reached out to His people—and how they tried (and often failed) to reach back. Here's the big picture.

In the Beginning

(Genesis 1–11)

The Bible begins by telling us how the world came into existence and how human beings became separated from God. This part of the Bible tells the story of Creation, the first murder, the start of different languages at the Tower of Babel, and the flood, which God used to bring judgment on the people who had turned away from Him.

Stories of the First People

(Genesis 12–50 and the book of Job)

Abraham was chosen by God to be the father of a great nation. God's chosen people would be called to do His will on earth. Abraham had a son named Isaac, Isaac had a son named Jacob, and Jacob had *twelve* sons, whose children would one day form the twelve tribes of Israel. These twelve sons and their families went to Egypt to save themselves from a deadly famine, but they eventually became slaves in the land.

Time to Leave Egypt

(Exodus–Joshua)

God called Moses to lead His chosen people out of their slavery in Egypt and into the Promised Land. But once they were on their way, the Israelites didn't always obey God's laws. God punished their disobedience by making them spend 40 years wandering in the desert. When their wanderings were over, they finally conquered the Promised Land under the leadership of Joshua.

Dark Times for Israel

(Judges–Ruth)

God provided wise judges to lead the people of Israel during the dark days when the Israelites kept forgetting His law and worshipping other gods instead. Just as things would begin to improve, the people would fall back into sin. This pattern repeated itself again and again, but God kept reaching out to His people and reminding them to obey His law.

Long Live the Kings!

(1 Samuel–2 Chronicles, as well as Psalms, Proverbs, Ecclesiastes, Song of Songs, and some of the books of the prophets)

The nation of Israel wasn't supposed to need a king. *God*

was their king. The Israelites wanted to be like other nations, though, and God finally gave them what they wanted: a human king. This first king, Saul, was a failure. Two good kings, David and Solomon, followed him. But after Solomon died, Israel split into two nations—Israel in the north and Judah in the south. Both kingdoms suffered under evil rulers and sank into sin and disobedience.

Captives!

(Ezra, Nehemiah, and some of the books of the prophets)

Because God's people continued to disobey Him, He punished them by removing them from the Promised Land. The temple and the city of Jerusalem were destroyed as a punishment for the people's sins. God's people were not allowed to return to their home for 70 years. When they finally returned from captivity, their first job was to rebuild the temple.

The Time of Silence

For 400 years between the end of the Old Testament and the beginning of the New Testament, God didn't speak to His people through prophets. Toward the end of this time, the Jews lived under Roman rule.

Jesus Comes to Earth

(Matthew–John)

God Himself entered the world as a little baby, Jesus Christ, to fulfill the promise He had made with Israel and to invite all people everywhere into His kingdom. Jesus told stories, healed the sick, performed miracles, and was crucified on a cross for the salvation of all people. But that wasn't the end! Jesus rose from the dead and went up into heaven, and He promised that someday He would come back again.

What the First Christians Did

(Acts–Revelation)

Through the power of the Holy Spirit, Jesus helped His disciples carry on His message and establish the church, which is His body on earth. After the Gospels (Matthew, Mark, Luke, John), most of the rest of the books of the New Testament are letters to churches that addressed problems they were facing and gave instructions about living in Christ. They also encouraged Christians to look forward to the time when Jesus would come again.

That's the big story. Now, in the pages that follow, we'll take a quick look at what's in each and every book of the Bible and point out some of the most exciting stories and passages in each one. Let's jump into the adventure of exploring the whole Bible, book by book. When we're done, you'll have a good idea of what's in the Bible and where to find some of the most famous stories.

The Old Testament

Can you find the names of the books of the Old Testament, which are hidden in this puzzle? Remember that the names you are looking for can be hidden across, backward, up, down, and diagonally. When you find a name, circle it.

```
J E R E M I A H M Y   L R O N U M B E R S
S O C M Z H P R O V E R B S U A F W A P X O L M
J B C D R O V K L Y U Z Q H T R P S L M J T E L
U A L Y A S R Q U A F P N E H E M I A H O L V S
D D E U T E R O N O M Y D S A R O G C X N S I G
G I S A I A H T M D Z E P H A N I A H P A I T N
E A I M B Q T Y N I E L N A T S M Z I O H C I L
S H A B A K K U K A C O M T E S T H E R D L C G
J O S H U A I D W T H A G G A I L S P U S W U E
K O T A L S N A R Q A U H D L T J T J S L I S N
G L E R M B G N E U R T M A L I I G H R A P A E
I P S L J U S I K M I F E R C H R O N I C L E S
E X O D U S E E T L A N X A L V S E N R K W M I
D E Z E K I E L G R H R J S O N G O F S O N G S
```

GENESIS	NEHEMIAH	HOSEA
EXODUS	ESTHER	JOEL
LEVITICUS	JOB	AMOS
NUMBERS	PSALMS	OBADIAH
DEUTERONOMY	PROVERBS	JONAH
JOSHUA	ECCLESIASTES	MICAH
JUDGES	SONG OF SONGS	NAHUM
RUTH	ISAIAH	HABAKKUK
SAMUEL	JEREMIAH	ZEPHANIAH
KINGS	LAMENTATIONS	HAGGAI
CHRONICLES	EZEKIEL	ZECHARIAH
EZRA	DANIEL	MALACHI

Bible Basics for Kids

A Tour of the Bible, Book by Book

The Old Testament
Genesis

Genesis goes back to the very beginning of time. When there was nothing at all—not even space—God created everything we see. He filled space with galaxies, filled the oceans with water and sharks and sea turtles, filled the rainforests with trees and moss and frogs, and filled the deserts with sand dunes and camels. In the blink of an eye, God made time, goldfish, spiders, rainbows, and the tallest pine trees!

This is a book that answers the really big questions people ask about the world. *Where did we come from? Why are we here? Why is there so much pain and evil in the world?* But Genesis doesn't answer these questions the way we might expect, with facts and figures and long-winded scientific explanations. Instead, it answers our questions by telling stories.

And these stories are full of action! We've got the creation of the whole universe, romance, jealousy, battles, famine, trickery, and above all, God reaching out to His beloved sons and daughters. He shows them how much He cares and teaches them how to live. They don't always pay attention, though. Sometimes they get angry or jealous. Sometimes they don't obey the simplest commands. Sometimes they bully people who are weak. Sometimes they fight with their brothers and sisters.

Does any of that sound familiar? God is reaching out to you the same way He reached out to Adam and Eve, Noah, and Abraham. Genesis is just the beginning of the journey.

Don't Miss This!
Creation (Genesis 1)
The Fall (Genesis 3)
Noah and the Flood (Genesis 6–8)
The Tower of Babel (Genesis 11)
The Call of Abraham (Genesis 12)
Jacob Wrestles with an Angel (Genesis 32)
Joseph Saves Egypt from Famine (Genesis 41)

Exodus

Exodus begins 400 years after the story of Genesis ends. In that time, the Egyptians have forgotten all about Joseph saving them during the famine. They've made the Israelites their slaves. God chose a man named Moses to deliver His people from slavery and bring them to the Promised Land.

Moses thought God had chosen the wrong man. He was afraid to speak to Pharaoh and wanted to give the responsibility to someone else. But God gave Moses the strength he needed.

Has God ever asked you to do something you thought was too hard for you? If so, you'll understand exactly how Moses felt. But when God asks you to do something—even something hard—He'll always give you the strength and courage to do it!

Don't Miss This!

God Speaks to Moses from the Burning Bush (Exodus 3)
The Ten Plagues and the Escape from Egypt (Exodus 7–14)
The Ten Commandments (Exodus 20)

THE TEN COMMANDMENTS

1. You shall have no other gods before me.

2. You shall not make for yourself an idol.

3. You shall not misuse the name of the LORD your God.

4. Remember the Sabbath day by keeping it holy.

5. Honor your father and your mother.

6. You shall not murder.

7. You shall not commit adultery.

8. You shall not steal.

9. You shall not give false testimony against your neighbor.

10. You shall not covet.

Joseph: From Slave to Ruler

Genesis 37, 39–50

Can you find the words that are hidden in this puzzle from the list at the bottom of this page? Remember that the words you are looking for can be hidden across, backward, up, down, and diagonally. When you find a word, circle it.

```
J A C O B E S J O E R G R A I N R
R S W C R W T G M E G Y P T Y J Y
L V S T O R E H O U S E R H R S D
P I T N T L N M U A E N I E T E R
S Q N E H S O G R B R G S L A V E
W X A S E K U R N U V I O Q L E A
O P H A R A O H E N Y P N U V N M
C U C T S E C O N D R U L E R Y S
T Y R P O T I P H A R S W I F E M
A H E U D I T H I N C O W S T A P
F A M I N E W D M C H R B T I R O
S U O L A E J O S E P H D E R S E
```

ABUNDANCE	GRAIN	POTIPHARS WIFE
BROTHERS	JACOB	PRISON
COLORED ROBE	JEALOUS	SECOND RULER
DREAMS	JOSEPH	SEVEN YEARS
EGYPT	MERCHANTS	SLAVE
FAMINE	MOURN	STOREHOUSE
FAT COWS	PHARAOH	THIN COWS
GOSHEN	PIT	

Leviticus

Rules, rules, rules. Clean your room. Wash your hands. Look both ways. Eat your vegetables. Sometimes it seems like rules are all you ever hear.

Rules are important, though. They give us guidance and teach us the right way to live. Just as parents and teachers give you rules for your protection, God gave His people a set of laws to live by. There are rules about which foods are good to eat and which foods you should avoid. There are rules about what clothes you can wear, who can be priests, and how we should treat the poor. Some of those rules sound pretty strange to us today, but they helped God's people live in peace and harmony with one another.

Don't Miss This!
The First Priests (Leviticus 8)
The Holy Days and Festivals (Leviticus 23)

Numbers

Have you ever gone to a family reunion? You get to see all your aunts, uncles, cousins, grandparents...maybe even great-grandparents. Maybe you took a picture of the whole family so you could remember who was there.

The book of Numbers is like a picture at a family reunion. It's a snapshot of all the people who lived in the family of God. There are long lists of names in this book, but there are also spies, battles, and even a talking donkey! It's an exciting time for the Israelites: After 40 years of wandering in the desert, they're finally getting ready to enter the Promised Land.

The Spies' Report (Numbers 13–14)
Balaam and the Donkey (Numbers 22)
Joshua Appointed as Leader (Numbers 27)

Deuteronomy

Have you ever had to say goodbye to someone? A forever goodbye? Maybe someone you loved was dying. Maybe a friend was moving away. If you knew it was the last time you were going to see that person, you wouldn't waste any time. You'd say the truest and most important words of all: *I love you.*

Moses is getting old, and he knows it's time for him to die. He has a few more things to say to God's people, though—the truest and most important words of all. *God loves you.* The book of Deuteronomy is Moses's farewell message to the Israelites. He reminds them of the covenant God made with them. God is the one true God, Moses says. He will watch over us and protect us, His people, and in return He asks for our worship and obedience.

Moses Teaches About God's Love (Deuteronomy 6–7)
God's Concern for the Needy (Deuteronomy 15)
Moses's Death (Deuteronomy 32–34)

48   Bible Basics for Kids

Joshua

Ever been on a long car ride you thought would never end? Imagine how the Israelites felt after wandering in the desert for 40 years! After escaping from slavery in Egypt, they had finally, finally, *finally* reached the Promised Land...but there was just one problem. Someone else was already living there.

The book of Joshua is the story of how God helped the Israelites conquer the land of Canaan. As usual, the Israelites don't always do exactly what God says. They mess up a lot. But God is always there to shepherd His people.

Don't Miss This!
Rahab and the Spies (Joshua 2)
The Battle of Jericho (Joshua 6)
The Sun Stands Still (Joshua 10)
Joshua's Farewell Message and Death (Joshua 23–24)

Judges

After Joshua died, God's people still needed a leader. They needed someone to remind them of God's Word and help them live according to His laws. So God sent judges—people like Deborah, Samson, and Gideon—to rule and guide the Israelites.

The people didn't always listen, though, just like we don't always listen to pastors and teachers today. The Israelites fought and sinned and disobeyed. A *lot*. The whole book of

Judges can be summed up in its very last verse: "In those days Israel had no king; everyone did as they saw fit."

Don't Miss This!
Deborah (Judges 4–5)
Gideon (Judges 6–8)
Samson (Judges 13–16)

Ruth

The book of Ruth contains one of the world's most beautiful love stories. (But don't worry—there's not too much mushy stuff!)

The story takes place "in the days when the judges ruled"—during the time of all that violence and warfare and disobedience we just read about in Judges. Ruth is a young woman whose husband died. Because of her devotion to her mother-in-law, Naomi, she travels with her to Bethlehem. They don't know how they'll survive, where they'll find food, or where they'll sleep at night. But God is about to intervene in the most astonishing way.

Have you ever felt like you didn't know where to turn? Like your situation was hopeless...and then God showed up to take care of you after all? If you have, you'll understand just how Ruth felt when she got to Bethlehem. This isn't just some sappy love story. It's a story about God going to any length to take care of the children He loves.

Don't Miss This!
The Kinsman-Redeemer (Ruth 3)

First Samuel

Have you ever shown up at school and discovered that everyone was wearing an armful of Silly Bandz...except you? Or maybe everyone was playing with a hacky sack...except you. Or everyone had died their hair purple...except you! You wanted to follow the trend, right? You wanted to have what everyone else had.

The Israelites would have known exactly how you felt. They wanted what all the other nations around them had: a king. The book of First Samuel is the story of how God finally gave them what they wanted, even though He knew it wasn't what was best. The prophet Samuel anoints Saul as king, but Saul doesn't remain faithful to God. God has a different king in mind: a young shepherd boy named David.

Don't Miss This!
The People Demand a King (1 Samuel 8)
David and Goliath (1 Samuel 17)
David and Jonathan (1 Samuel 18–20)

Second Samuel

When God called David to be the king of Israel, he wasn't much older than you. Second Samuel is the story of how David grew up to be the greatest king of Israel. The Bible calls him "a man after [God's] own heart," but he sure isn't perfect. He makes a lot of mistakes. He steals another man's wife. He commits a murder to cover it up. His own children rebel against him. As you read, look for all the times David messes up but learns to repent—and watch how God uses even the big mistakes for good.

Don't Miss This!
David and Bathsheba (2 Samuel 11–12)
The Death of Absalom (2 Samuel 18)

First Kings

Who's the wisest person you've ever met? Your grandma, maybe? What about your pastor? Or your parents? Maybe a teacher?

Solomon, King David's son, was the wisest person who ever lived. But he made a couple of really dumb decisions. He married lots of different women, and some of those women didn't worship God. Instead, they told the Israelites about other gods—fake gods. God sent prophets like Elijah to remind His people to worship Him alone.

After King Solomon died, the Israelites did a lot of arguing and fighting. No one agreed on who the next king should be. The fighting got so bad that the nation of Israel divided into two countries—Israel in the north and Judah in the south. Many kings ruled Israel and Judah after Solomon. Some of them tried to follow God, but most of them were evil.

Don't Miss This!
The Wisdom of Solomon (1 Kings 3–4)
The Queen of Sheba (1 Kings 10)
The Kingdom Divided (1 Kings 12)
Ahab and Jezebel (1 Kings 16–22)
Elijah on Mount Carmel (1 Kings 18)

Second Kings

The book of Second Kings is the story of a nation in danger. Many different kings ruled over Israel and Judah, and all but a few of them encouraged the Israelites to worship false gods. God was angry with His people. For so many years He'd been telling them the right way to live, and the people kept turning away. The Bible tells us, "They did wicked things that aroused the LORD's anger" (2 Kings 17:11).

The book ends with other nations coming and taking the Israelites into captivity. Because of their disobedience, God's people were slaves again—just like they had been in Egypt.

Don't Miss This!
Elijah and the Chariot to Heaven (2 Kings 2)
The Ministry of Elisha (2 Kings 2–6)
Israel Destroyed (2 Kings 17)
Josiah's Reforms (2 Kings 22–23)
Judah Destroyed (2 Kings 25)

First Chronicles

This book tells the same stories as Second Samuel, but from a different point of view. This book was probably written just after the Israelites returned from captivity. First Chronicles was a reminder of Israel's "good old days"—the days when the people worshipped the one true God. In this book we don't read about all of David's mistakes. We're reminded of all the good things he did and the ways he and the Israelites pleased God.

Second Chronicles

This book continues the story of David and Solomon. In Second Chronicles, you'll read all about the temple Solomon built to honor God. The writer also includes stories of the wicked kings. He wanted the Israelites to remember the good times, but also warn them of the dangers of not obeying God.

Ezra

God's people have been in exile for decades—about as long as your grandparents have been alive! But remember: No matter how much they've sinned, God will never leave His people without hope. The Israelites are set free from their captivity and return to their homeland. And what's the very first thing they do? Rebuild the temple—the place where they worship God.

Nehemiah

The Israelites had a big job on their hands. It was time to rebuild the wall around Jerusalem...and it was a ton of work. Too much for any one person—or even a hundred people.

Fortunately, God sent Nehemiah to inspire the Israelites. He motivated and encouraged them, helped them carry out their plans, and reminded them of the laws God gave them to live by.

Have you ever faced a huge task and needed help to finish it? Maybe you needed a parent to sit down and help you figure it out, or maybe you needed a friend to say, "I know you can do it!" You can ask God to send you a Nehemiah—someone who will help you finish the job God has given you.

Don't Miss This!
Rebuilding the Walls (Nehemiah 4–6)
Reading the Law and Confession of Sin (Nehemiah 8–9)

Esther

Have you ever had to keep a secret? A really big secret? Maybe your dad is planning a surprise for your mom and doesn't want you to tell her. Maybe you know who your friend has a crush on.

Esther, the queen of Persia, had a secret too. But this wasn't just any secret. If someone found out what she was hiding, she would be killed.

Esther is the story of a very brave, intelligent, and faithful young woman caught in a sticky situation. This is a book filled with danger and suspense as a queen tries to rescue her people from an evil plot. And God, as always, is working behind the scenes to take care of the people He loves.

Don't Miss This!

Esther's Courage (Esther 4–5)

The Feast of Purim (Esther 9)

Job

Job was having a bad day. A *really* bad day. A band of raiders killed his servants. His livestock were lost in a fire. And then came the news that a house had collapsed on his children, and all of them had died.

Most of us have never experienced suffering like that. But we all have days when trouble comes. We all have times when our hearts hurt, and no matter how hard we cry nothing seems to get any better. Tears can't make your grandpa stop dying. Tears can't give your dad his job back. Tears can't make your parents stay married.

In those tough times, we want to yell at God. We want to ask if He's even paying attention. In the book of Job, God speaks directly to a man who is suffering. He doesn't say, "Time heals all wounds." He doesn't say, "Everything happens for a reason." His answer is far more mysterious—and far more wonderful—than that.

Don't Miss This!
Job's Testing (Job 1–2)
God Speaks (Job 38–41)
Job's Confession and Restoration (Job 42)

Psalms

Have you ever been so happy you could sing? Or so angry you could just spit? Have you ever felt so forlorn that you wanted to cry? So lonely that you didn't know where to turn? So joyful that the laughter just bubbled right out of you?

So had King David. The book of Psalms is a collection of songs that David and other musicians wrote to God. These prayers and poems are filled with emotion, showing us that it's okay to be excited, impatient, frustrated, anxious, in despair, or full of delight. There's a psalm to fit every one of your feelings. When you want to talk to God but aren't sure how to start, the Psalms are a great place to begin.

Are you trying to tell God you trust Him no matter what? Check out Psalm 13.

Do you need help and aren't sure where you can turn? Try Psalm 42.

Do you need to tell God you're sorry? Read Psalm 51.

Are you feeling afraid? Turn to Psalm 91.

Is your heart overflowing with thankfulness? Check out Psalm 100.

Do you need reassurance? Try Psalm 121.

Do you ever wonder if God could really care about you? Read Psalm 139.

Don't Miss This!
The Lord Is My Shepherd (Psalm 23)
Trust in God (Psalm 27)
The Word of God (Psalm 119)
Worship and Praise (Psalm 150)

Proverbs

Life isn't about the destination. It's about the journey.
Do one thing every day that scares you.
Actions speak louder than words.

Maybe you've heard a parent or teacher say a proverb like that. Proverbs are good advice or wise sayings. But did you know there's a whole *book* of proverbs in the Bible?

King Solomon was the wisest person who ever lived, and this book is full of his (and a few others') practical tips and advice about things like choosing good friends, having compassion toward the needy, and being careful what you say. The most important lesson is this: "The fear of the LORD is the beginning of wisdom" (Proverbs 9:10).

Proverbs to Remember

Trust in the LORD with all your heart and lean not on your own understanding; in all your ways submit to him, and he will make your paths straight *(Proverbs 3:5-6)*.

Above all else, guard your heart, for everything you do flows from it *(Proverbs 4:23)*.

Do not rebuke mockers or they will hate you; rebuke the wise and they will love you. Instruct the wise and they will be wiser still; teach the righteous and they will add to their learning *(Proverbs 9:8-9)*.

Those who guard their lips preserve their lives, but those who speak rashly will come to ruin *(Proverbs 13:3)*.

Whoever is patient has great understanding, but one who is quick-tempered displays folly *(Proverbs 14:29)*.

A gentle answer turns away wrath, but a harsh word stirs up anger *(Proverbs 15:1)*.

Plans fail for lack of counsel, but with many advisers they succeed *(Proverbs 15:22)*.

Pride goes before destruction, a haughty spirit before a fall *(Proverbs 16:18)*.

Let someone else praise you, and not your own mouth; an outsider, and not your own lips *(Proverbs 27:2)*.

As water reflects the face, so one's life reflects the heart *(Proverbs 27:19)*.

Ecclesiastes

I've got the joy, joy, joy, joy down in my heart.
If you're happy and you know it…
This is the day the Lord has made. We will rejoice and be glad in it!

Sounds like if you have Jesus in your heart, you're supposed to be happy all the time. Right?

Not necessarily. The book of Ecclesiastes says it's normal to feel that life is unfair sometimes—even meaningless. But a life lived for God gives us meaning, wisdom, and purpose, even if it doesn't guarantee that everything will go right.

Don't Miss This!
A Time for Everything (Ecclesiastes 3)
Serve God While You Are Young (Ecclesiastes 11–12)

Song of Songs

Roses are red, violets are blue…

Have you ever had a crush? Maybe you were totally in love? So in love that you wrote a poem?

Song of Songs is one of the world's oldest love poems. A bride and groom are getting married, and now they get to celebrate a special kind of love. This book is all about that special, joyful love. The bride and groom share their excitement, tenderness, and pleasure at being together. This love goes way beyond red roses and blue violets. Love in marriage is a picture of how much God loves His people and would do anything to save them…even die for them.

Isaiah

Isaiah was a prophet in Judah during the reigns of four kings, and his job was to warn each king of the threat posed by foreign nations. But in the midst of those threats of judgment, he also gave a message of hope, looking beyond the suffering right in front of them and toward the reign of the coming Messiah, who would save God's people from their sins. The book is filled with powerful words and beautiful images, and it reminds us that salvation comes from God alone.

Jeremiah

Ever feel like no one was listening to you? Maybe you had a good idea but no one paid any attention. The prophet Jeremiah would have known exactly how you felt: He had a very important message, but he couldn't find anyone to listen to him. Because of that, some people call him "the weeping prophet."

What was the message no one listened to? Judgment was coming. God's people were sinning so badly that He had to punish them. Jeremiah reminded the people that the Potter (God) wished to shape the clay (God's people—just like you) into what He intended for them. That's a message that's still important today. How is God trying to shape you?

Don't Miss This!
The Potter and the Clay (Jeremiah 18)
The New Covenant (Jeremiah 31)

Lamentations

When was the last time you were really, really sad? What did you do? Did you cry? Did you tell someone how much you were hurting? Did you pray?

Lamentations is the prayer of Jeremiah. He wasn't just sad; he was in agony. Jerusalem, God's holy city, had been destroyed by enemy nations. In this prayer, Jeremiah begs for God's forgiveness and calls the Israelites to rededicate themselves to the Lord. This book reminds us that we can talk to God in any situation—even when we're suffering and don't think there's any hope.

Don't Miss This!
A Reminder of God's Faithfulness (Lamentations 3)

Ezekiel

Ezekiel was a prophet sent by God to preach to the Israelites while they were in exile. And some of his preaching looked pretty weird! He lay on his side for 390 days just to prove a point. He ate only one meal a day...and he cooked it over manure. He smashed pottery and told the people about incredible symbolic visions God had given him.

Why did he do all this? To remind God's people that salvation was coming. To many people watching him, Ezekiel must have seemed crazy, but his message was one of hope.

Don't Miss This!
A Vision of God's Glory (Ezekiel 1–3)
The Valley of Dry Bones (Ezekiel 37)
The Future Heavenly Temple (Ezekiel 40–48)

Daniel

What if everyone was doing something you knew was wrong? Would you go along with it? Or would you stand up for what you knew was right?

Daniel is the story of a young man not much older than you who faced that very question. Should he eat food that God had forbidden? Should he stop praying to the one true God? Should he bow down to a golden statue instead? The book of Daniel is the incredible story of God coming to rescue His children even when there doesn't seem to be any way out.

Don't Miss This!
The Fiery Furnace (Daniel 3)
Daniel in the Lions' Den (Daniel 6)

Hosea

What would you do if a friend was mean to you? Maybe they betrayed a secret or went behind your back. Would you forgive them?

What if they did it again? Would you still be their friend? What if they did it a third time? Or a fourth? You probably wouldn't want to be their friend anymore.

The book of Hosea is a picture of God's patient love for His people. That love doesn't change no matter what we do. It's the same even when we don't deserve it. Even when we turn our backs on God again and again and again, He will still reach out to us and wrap us in His loving embrace.

Don't Miss This!
Hosea and Gomer (Hosea 1–3)
God's Love for Israel (Hosea 11)
A Hopeful Future (Hosea 14)

Joel

When you do something wrong, your parents will forgive you. But first you'll have to face the consequences for disobeying. Your parents will punish you, even though they love you. It's the same with God: He loves His people, but they can't keep sinning without facing the Lord's judgment.

In this book, the prophet Joel warns God's people that punishment for their sins is coming. But even with this punishment comes the hope that they will be restored to Him.

Don't Miss This!
The Day of the Lord (Joel 2)

Amos

"I can name all the books of the Bible in order. I bet you can't do that."

"I got a better grade on my Bible memory work than you did."

"I think God answered my prayer because I never forget to do my devotions."

Sound familiar? It's easy to get prideful about our relationship with God. Sometimes we use our faith to make others feel bad...and God doesn't like that one little bit.

Things were no different back in Israel, so God sent a prophet named Amos to preach to the people. Amos had strong words about the Israelites' pride and how they liked to show off when they worshipped. God, Amos said, doesn't like it when we pretend to love Him just to impress someone else. He also spoke out against the injustice that left the poor forgotten and oppressed. How can we claim to be faithful followers of God but neglect the people who need Him most?

Don't Miss This!
A Call to Repentance (Amos 5)
A Warning to the Rich (Amos 6)

Obadiah

The Israelites weren't the only ones who ignored God's laws. The Edomites, neighbors of Israel, also sinned and had to face God's punishment. The short little book of Obadiah is a warning that calls the people to repent, confess their sins, and turn back to God.

Jonah

Have you ever really, really, *really* not wanted to go somewhere? Maybe you were dreading a dentist appointment. Maybe you didn't want to go with your mom to her friend's house because you knew her son was a bully.

Maybe you even thought about running away.

So did Jonah.

The people of Nineveh were rebelling against God and acting like bullies toward the Israelites. They weren't worshipping God or following His commandments. God told His prophet Jonah to go to Nineveh and remind the people about Him. But Jonah didn't want to go. He wanted God to destroy these enemies of Israel. So he decided to run away...but you can never run away from God.

Don't Miss This!
Jonah and the Big Fish (Jonah 1–2)

Micah

God sent the prophet Micah to speak out against injustice. God desires more from us than just thinking holy thoughts or saying holy words, says Micah. We are also called to care for those in need. Micah gives us a glimpse of the glorious future when the Lord will gather His people in a kingdom ruled by the Messiah.

Don't Miss This!
Judgment on Those Who Are Mean to the Poor (Micah 3)

Nahum

Remember Jonah? More than 100 years after his missionary trip in the big fish, the people of Nineveh had once again forgotten God. Nahum was sent to warn them that God had nearly had it with them. But along with his message of warning, Nahum reminds the people that God is slow to anger and abounding in love.

Don't Miss This!
A Psalm of God's Majesty (Nahum 1)

Habakkuk

It was a dark time in Judah. God's people were suffering, but instead of helping each other, they became violent and persecuted those who were most in need. And there, on the horizon, the Babylonians were waiting to invade. Habakkuk, one of God's prophets, asks God a question: "Why did You allow all this pain?" God's answer is simple: The people are being judged for their sins.

But the Babylonians aren't any holier than the Israelites. God says that they too will be punished for what they have done wrong. Habakkuk finishes with a prayer of faith and trust.

Don't Miss This!
The Righteous Will Live by Faith (Habakkuk 2)

Zephaniah

The prophet Zephaniah brought God's word to the people during the reign of Josiah. He assured them that Judah would be judged for their sins, but he also looked forward to the coming day of the Lord. Josiah was one of the few kings who followed God's law, so Zephaniah's message seems to have gotten through.

Don't Miss This!
Israel Will Be Restored (Zephaniah 3)

Haggai

After the exile, Haggai returned to Jerusalem and found that the people were sad. Life was so difficult that they had stopped rebuilding the temple. Haggai reminded the people that the temple (just like the church) is more than just a building. It's a sign that the land is dedicated to God. If we put God first, we will experience His blessings.

Don't Miss This!
The Prophecy of the Temple (Haggai 2)

Zechariah

Like Haggai, Zechariah preached to the discouraged Jews who had returned from exile in Babylon. But instead of focusing on the current problems, Zechariah had a series of eight strange visions about the future. No one knows exactly what these visions mean, but we do know he was talking about the coming Messiah, Jesus, who would save the people from their sins. When Zechariah speaks of this glorious future, he can barely contain his excitement.

Don't Miss This!
The Wounded Shepherd (Zechariah 12–13)

Malachi

Are you noticing a pattern in the prophets' messages? God is serious about the consequences of sin and disobedience! It's easy to neglect our worship and our responsibilities as God's children, but Malachi reminds us to stay true to Him and follow His ways.

Don't Miss This!
The People's Sin (Malachi 3)

The New Testament

Can you find the names of the books of the New Testament, which are hidden in this puzzle? Remember that the names you are looking for can be hidden across, backward, up, down, and diagonally. When you find a name, circle it.

```
T H W R T B R G M   O M J M P E T E R
E P H E S I A N S G S W B A Z D Y N M I E L
O H L E B T E J C R P J S T A L O G P Y V A
C I J V S U H A B U H V I T G B D J U D E G
H L O R G S I C O R I N T H I A N S M A L B
C E F L U D A O M S L K I E E L G J D O A T
J M A R K I E L D A I E L W O B Q U I S T I
K O B S R M T O O Q P R X Y S J R S E L I M
I N H Y L U Q S I N P A E T J X O E O N O O
T U B N L E O S D J I W C O N J M R W H N T
J I G F K O S I L E A A H E D I A N L S A H
P Q U U Y G D A H O N T N H E F N M I S R Y
G A L A T I A N S M S Y R S O J S Q E R D L
E P I S T L E S O F J O H N G U E V I S J L
```

MATTHEW
MARK
LUKE
JOHN
ACTS
ROMANS
CORINTHIANS

GALATIANS
EPHESIANS
PHILIPPIANS
COLOSSIANS
THESSALONIANS
TIMOTHY
TITUS

PHILEMON
HEBREWS
JAMES
PETER
EPISTLES OF JOHN
JUDE
REVELATION

The New Testament
Matthew

God's people had been waiting a long time for the Messiah. The prophets told stories about what He would be like, and the Gospel of Matthew shows that all those stories had come true in Jesus Christ!

Matthew looks at the life and death of Jesus from a Jewish point of view, connecting the events of His life with the people's hopes and expectations. The book begins with a family tree that proves Jesus's royal heritage. Matthew wants to make his point clear: Jesus of Nazareth is the longed-for Messiah, the One who ushers in the kingdom of God.

Don't Miss This!
The Birth of Jesus (Matthew 1–2)
The Sermon on the Mount (Matthew 5–7)
The Resurrection (Matthew 28)
The Great Commission (Matthew 28)

THE BEATITUDES

Blessed are the **poor in spirit**,
    for theirs is the **kingdom of heaven**.

Blessed are those who **mourn**,
    for they will be **comforted**.

Blessed are the **meek**,
    for they will **inherit the earth**.

Blessed are those who **hunger and
      thirst for righteousness**,
    for they will **be filled**.

Blessed are the **merciful**,
    for they will be **shown mercy**.

Blessed are the **pure in heart**,
    for they **will see God**.

Blessed are the **peacemakers**,
    for they will be called **children of God**.

Blessed are those who are **persecuted**
    because of righteousness,
    for theirs is the **kingdom of heaven**.

Bible Basics for Kids

Mark

When you're excited to tell a story, you can't wait to get it out. Mark was excited to tell people about Jesus. In this Gospel, Mark doesn't worry about explaining Jesus's family history or the details of His birth. He just jumps right into the story of Jesus's ministry.

This Gospel is fast-paced and full of action. You get the sense that Mark was out of breath when he wrote it. In Mark, you'll read stories about Jesus healing the sick, performing miracles, and teaching people about the kingdom of God.

Don't Miss This!
The Death of John the Baptist (Mark 6)
Jesus Walks on Water (Mark 6)
The Cost of Following Jesus (Mark 10)

Luke

If you have an unbelievable story to tell, someone might raise an eyebrow and say, "Really? Prove it!" They'll ask for details and evidence that prove your story is true.

Luke was writing the story of Jesus for people who were doubtful. He gives lots of details that prove his story is accurate and trustworthy. Luke shows us that Jesus didn't come just to save the Jews but to save *everyone*. He also discusses Jesus's concerns for the outcasts of society—the poor, the discouraged, the sick, and the suffering. To them, Jesus brings a message of hope and the love of a heavenly Father.

THE PARABLES OF JESUS

The Wise and Foolish Builders *(Matthew 7:24-27; Luke 6:47-49)*

The Sower and the Seeds *(Matthew 13:3-23; Mark 4:3-20; Luke 8:5-15)*

The Pearl of Great Price *(Matthew 13:45-46)*

The Lost Sheep *(Matthew 18:12-14; Luke 15:3-7)*

The Unmerciful Servant *(Matthew 18:23-35)*

The Workers in the Vineyard *(Matthew 20:1-16)*

The Two Sons *(Matthew 21:28-32)*

The Tenants *(Matthew 21:33-44; Mark 12:1-11; Luke 20:9-18)*

The Wedding Banquet *(Matthew 22:1-14)*

The Fig Tree (*Matthew 24:32-35; Mark 13:28-29; Luke 21:29-31*)

The Faithful and Wise Servant (*Matthew 24:45-51; Luke 12:42-48*)

The Ten Virgins (*Matthew 25:1-13*)

The Bags of Gold (*Matthew 25:14-30; Luke 19:12-27*)

The Sheep and the Goats (*Matthew 25:31-46*)

The Good Samaritan (*Luke 10:30-37*)

The Rich Fool (*Luke 12:16-21*)

The Great Banquet (*Luke 14:16-24*)

The Lost Coin (*Luke 15:8-10*)

The Prodigal Son (*Luke 15:11-32*)

The Rich Man and Lazarus (*Luke 16:19-31*)

The Persistent Widow (*Luke 18:1-8*)

John

The first three Gospels tell similar stories, but John's Gospel is different from the others. John is more thoughtful, exploring the deepest mysteries of who Jesus was and why He came. This book shows us that Jesus is fully God, and He came to earth to take our sins upon Himself. We deserve death and judgment, but Christ takes our place on the cross and, in return, gives us life and glory. As you read, count all the times Jesus says "I am" and listen to the things He says about Himself.

Don't Miss This!

In the Beginning (John 1)
Jesus and Nicodemus (John 3)
Jesus and the Samaritan Woman (John 4)
The Crucifixion and Resurrection (John 19–20)

THE GREAT "I AM" STATEMENTS OF JESUS

I am the **Bread of Life** (*John 6:35,48*)

I am the **Light of the World** (*John 8:12; 9:5*)

I am the **Gate** (*John 10:7,9*)

I am the **Good Shepherd** (*John 10:11,14*)

I am the **Resurrection and the Life** (*John 11:25*)

I am the **Way, the Truth, and the Life** (*John 14:6*)

The Gospel Message

John 3:16

```
                P D N L H B
                L N O E I N
                B H T S M K
                F E N V Y W
D U R S H P R T L P J H J P E Q W T
T O D O J N C Y R I D O N L Y N H E
F N T K A B L J S R E E T H I W A H
P E H L S T W G O D L V N E D F V C
M I G I O O R A N V H E E Y J R E L
S B C J F V M V J B M R J S T H A T
                E E T R Y H
                L D B H S I
                P M E W A P
                D E P E R T
                W O R L D L
                H J G I B L
                B L T Y S A
                U W R A H H
                T H E N D S
                W Q L D H B
```

FOR	HIS	HIM
GOD	ONE	SHALL
SO	AND	NOT
LOVED	ONLY	PERISH
THE	SON	BUT
WORLD	THAT	HAVE
THAT	WHOEVER	ETERNAL
HE	BELIEVES	LIFE
GAVE	IN	

Acts

Luke wasn't finished telling the story of Jesus. In the book of Acts, Luke tells us what happened after Jesus rose from the dead and was taken up to heaven. The disciples were filled with the Holy Spirit, and they had a new mission in life: to tell the whole world about the salvation Jesus brought to the world. It's a message that hasn't changed in 2,000 years.

In Acts, you'll read stories about Peter, the disciple who once denied that he even knew Jesus; Stephen, the first person to be killed for his beliefs; and Paul, the first missionary. Look for all the ways you see the Holy Spirit moving in this book. That same Spirit is still moving in the church—and in you—today!

Don't Miss This!
The Holy Spirit Comes at Pentecost (Acts 2)
Paul's Conversion (Acts 9)
Paul's Journey to Rome (Acts 27–28)

Romans

If you really want something, you have to pay for it, right? Not in God's eyes. The book of Romans tells us there's nothing we can do to earn God's love. We can never be good enough, righteous enough, or holy enough to deserve the salvation God gave us through Jesus Christ. We are all guilty of sin. But God made a way for us to be restored to a relationship with Him—a relationship so special we can call God *Daddy*. Nothing can ever separate us from God's love.

First Corinthians

The church at Corinth had a lot of problems...problems that sound familiar to us even today. The church struggled with disagreements, jealousy, and fighting. They weren't living by God's commands and they weren't taking worship seriously. That wasn't the way a church community was supposed to behave.

Paul wrote a letter to the church and pointed out that true Christians live by the power of the Holy Spirit, not by their own wants and desires. Paul reminded the people that we are all connected members of the Body of the Christ, and we all have gifts to offer one another.

Second Corinthians

Your babysitter says it's time to go to bed, and you want to stay up and play. So what do you do? Maybe you yell, "You're not my mom! You can't tell me what to do."

The people in the church at Corinth said something like

that to Paul after he sent his first letter. So in his second letter to the church, Paul defends his right to tell them how they should live, showing that God has made him a special leader in the church.

Paul also points out that the Christian life isn't always easy. Sometimes service to God can result in great suffering and bad treatment from other people.

Don't Miss This!
Paul's Thorn in the Flesh (2 Corinthians 12)

Galatians

If you're a Christian, you have to obey all the rules, right? You have to wear your hair a certain length. You can't go certain places or hang out with certain people. You have to...you should...you need to...

That attitude is called *legalism*, and the early church faced a lot of it. Because Jesus was a Jew, some people believed that all Christians had to follow the old Jewish laws. But Paul's response is clear: The gospel of Jesus is not about following laws and doing what's right. The gospel is about love and faith. Faith, says Paul, produces good works, but doing good won't save us. We can follow all the rules we want, but it won't get us into heaven. Only the saving grace of Christ will do that.

Don't Miss This!
Salvation by Faith (Galatians 2)
The Fruit of the Spirit (Galatians 5)

The Fruit of the Spirit

Galatians 5:22-23

Can you find the words that are hidden in this puzzle from the list at the bottom of this page? Remember that the words you are looking for can be hidden across, backward, up, down, and diagonally. When you find a word, circle it.

```
R H U O P Q R T K A C
S G D R S Y N L R N E
G Y J E K V N E J O W P X W U
B E L N L C I P P V K R P A S
F A I T H F U L N E S S A Q T
U T I L W E C N K P A C T B I
P S R E C T M O I B N C I L R
W D T N R W D F N U P W E D W
R C Y E D T M E D T I O N S P
T H P S G W K P N E R S C S Y
A R T S L N E H E L N O E G T
R D L V J P W R S J R D L H O
    G O O D N E S S N L R
    N E Y R D K O P W T D
```

FAITHFULNESS	JOY	PATIENCE
GENTLENESS	KINDNESS	PEACE
GOODNESS	LOVE	SELF CONTROL

Ephesians

Paul's letter to the Ephesians reminds us that not only are we chosen and loved by God, but the Holy Spirit gives us the power to live a new life in Christ. That new life is shown in a holy lifestyle, our family relationships, and our ability to stand up to the devil when he tries to make us do bad things. The letter gives us practical instructions for "walking in the Spirit."

Don't Miss This!
Our Position in Christ (Ephesians 1)
Marriage and Family Life (Ephesians 5–6)
The Armor of God (Ephesians 6)

Philippians

Have you ever won an award? Maybe a coach said you were the most valuable player. Maybe you gave the best piano recital. Maybe you read the most books in your whole class.

That made you feel pretty good, right? Maybe you were so excited that you bragged about your award.

Paul reminds us that whatever we're proud of is nothing compared to the joy of knowing Christ. He encourages us to keep striving to know Jesus better, because Jesus is the only Person worth bragging about.

Don't Miss This!
No Confidence in the Flesh (Philippians 3)
Rejoicing in Christ (Philippians 4)

Colossians

The gospel is awfully simple: If we have faith that Christ died to save us from our sins, we'll spend eternity with Him. For some people, that message is *too* simple. They want to find ways to make God's saving grace more complicated.

The book of Colossians is a letter from Paul reminding the church not to add extra laws onto the gospel. We won't be saved by following rules about what we can and cannot eat. We won't be saved by celebrating certain holidays. We'll be saved only by believing in Christ. Paul gives the church (and us) a strong reminder that Christianity is all about Christ—and Christ alone!

Don't Miss This!
Christ Is Lord (Colossians 1)
Christ Is Enough (Colossians 2)

First Thessalonians

Paul has lots of good things to say to the church in this letter. The Thessalonians have dedicated themselves to the truth, are sending out missionaries, and are conducting themselves well in the world. Paul doesn't want them to become discouraged, though, when people who don't believe in Christ do bad things to them. He reminds the church of our most blessed hope: Jesus is coming again!

Don't Miss This!
The Return of Christ (1 Thessalonians 4)

Second Thessalonians

As he did in his first letter, Paul comforts the Thessalonians with a reminder of Christ's promised return. However, he has to clear up some misunderstandings. Many Christians, thinking that Christ's return was just around the corner, had stopped working to earn a living. They had built their lives around waiting for Jesus to come back rather than staying focused on doing God's work in the world. God has given us an important mission, says Paul, and it's our job to carry it out.

Don't Miss This!
The Day of the Lord (2 Thessalonians 2)

First and Second Timothy

Paul wrote these two letters to a young church leader named Timothy. The pride Paul feels in this young man is very clear, but that doesn't stop him from offering some good advice and instruction on how to be a better pastor. By the time he writes the second letter, the relationship seems even closer. Paul encourages Timothy to "finish the race."

Don't Miss This!
Responsibility to Those in Need (1 Timothy 5)
Remaining Faithful (2 Timothy 3–4)

Titus

Like Timothy, Titus was a young church leader whom Paul encouraged and taught. In this letter Paul gives very specific guidelines about church leadership. Pastors and other leaders should be good people and have a good understanding of the church's teachings.

Don't Miss This!
The Ministry of a Pastor (Titus 2)

Philemon

Have you ever been so mad at someone—a friend, a brother, a sister—that you stopped talking to them? You stopped hanging out with them, stopped calling them, stopped wanting to be around them. But after a while, you missed your friend. You missed the good times you shared. You wanted to have a relationship again.

Paul knew two people in that same situation. Onesimus was a slave who had run away from his master, Philemon. Both of them became Christians through Paul's ministry, and Paul didn't want there to be any bitterness or resentment between them. In this letter, Paul asked them to forgive each other and be reconciled as brothers in Christ.

Hebrews

Many Jews had found faith in Jesus and become Christians. They still had a lot of questions, though. How does Christianity fit into the history of God and His people?

The author of this letter reviews the history of the Old Testament and shows that everything in Jewish tradition—priesthood, sacrifices, covenant, the Law—points to Jesus Christ. Jesus, says Hebrews, is the ultimate Prophet, Priest, and King.

James

Okay. So you believe in Jesus. Great.

Now what? How does being a Christian change the way you act? The way you spend your money? The way you treat people?

Those are questions the early Christians weren't sure how to answer. James, the brother of Jesus, answers them in this letter. He says that good works are the natural result of faith, and his letter is filled with advice about putting faith into action. James helps Christians think about how our faith is related to the way we speak and act.

First and Second Peter

Has anyone ever made fun of you for being a Christian? The Christians in the early church certainly knew how you felt. They weren't just being made fun of—they were being *killed* for their faith.

The apostle Peter knew all about suffering for the sake of the gospel. In these two letters, he encourages Christians to hold tight to their faith, no matter how difficult or dangerous it might be. He also reminds us that we can have hope even if we suffer, because Christ is coming again!

Don't Miss This!
The Purpose of Suffering (1 Peter 2–4)
The Danger of False Teaching (2 Peter 2)

First, Second, and Third John

Some people had funny ideas about Jesus and what it meant to be a Christian. The Gnostics were a group of people who believed what they did with their bodies didn't matter—only their eternal souls were important. The teachings of the Gnostics were a huge threat to the early Christians, who were still learning what it meant to live out their faith in Jesus. In these three letters, John shows that living a pure life in this world is hugely important. Love, he says, is the sign of a real and vibrant faith.

Don't Miss This!
Righteous Living and Love for God's Children (1 John 3–4)

Jude

The book of Jude is a brief letter written by a brother of James and Jesus. It's a reminder to stay true to the words of Jesus and not be fooled by false teaching. Jude calls believers to live holy lives and root themselves in the one true faith.

Revelation

When Jesus rose from the dead and ascended into heaven, He left us with a promise: He would come back to earth again. The book of Revelation is a vision of what that return will look like. Parts of it can be confusing. Even 2,000 years after it was written, Christians are still trying to figure out exactly what the vision means.

But here's the important part. When you know a story has a happy ending, you don't have to worry if there are scary parts in the middle. Revelation tells us that even though there's suffering and pain in the world today, someday Christ will conquer all the powers of evil and restore His kingdom on earth. That's a huge comfort to the early Christians and to believers today. In the book of Revelation, we see how the story will end—with God triumphing over the devil and creating a new heaven and a new earth where we will live with Him forever!

Don't Miss This!
Letters to the Seven Churches (Revelation 2–3)
The Vision of the Lamb (Revelation 4–5)
A New Heaven and a New Earth (Revelation 20–22)

More Ridiculous Bible Riddles

(See the answers on the next page)

1. Who was the greatest comedian in the Bible?

2. Why is Adam considered a famous runner?

3. What reason did Adam give his children for why they no longer lived in Eden?

4. The ark had a window on the top floor, but how did Noah get light down into the bottom floors?

5. Who was the greatest mathematician in the Bible?

6. Why couldn't anyone play cards on the ark?

7. Where was Solomon's temple located?

8. Who was the smallest man in the Bible?

9. What time of day was Adam created?

10. Why didn't Noah go fishing?

Answers to
More Ridiculous Bible Riddles

1. Samson. He brought down the house (Judges 16).

2. He was first in the human race.

3. "Your mother ate us out of house and home" (Genesis 3).

4. Flood lights (Genesis 6–8).

5. Moses, because he wrote the book of Numbers.

6. Because Noah was standing on the deck.

7. On the side of his forehead.

8. Peter, because he slept on his watch (Mark 14:32-38).

9. A little before Eve.

10. He had only two worms.

Part 3

HELP FOR EVERY DAY
FROM GOD'S WORD

Whispers from God

Sometimes you're overwhelmed with a situation and don't know where to turn.

Your best friend all of a sudden decides that you're not friends anymore...and she's going to tell the whole class all the embarrassing stories she knows about you.

Your uncle has cancer and your parents get all quiet when they talk about him, like something's really wrong.

You told a lie (like, a big one) and you thought you could get away with it. But now someone else is getting blamed—and punished—for your mistake.

What are you supposed to do? The Bible doesn't have anything to say about *this*, does it?

You'd be surprised! Reading the Bible is like hearing God whispering to you, helping you through those tough times and showing you that He loves you...

no matter what people say about you
no matter how far away He seems
no matter how much you've messed up

When you're facing tough times and you're not sure if God's paying attention, start listening to the whisper. He's always reaching out.

Verses for When **You Feel Afraid**

The LORD is my light and my salvation—
   whom shall I fear?
The LORD is the stronghold of my life—
   of whom shall I be afraid?

(Psalm 27:1)

In God I trust and am not afraid.
   What can man do to me?

(Psalm 56:11)

He will cover you with his feathers,
   and under his wings you will find refuge;
   his faithfulness will be your shield and
     rampart.
You will not fear the terror of night,
   nor the arrow that flies by day,
nor the pestilence that stalks in the darkness,
   nor the plague that destroys at midday.

(Psalm 91:4-6)

Have no fear of sudden disaster
   or of the ruin that overtakes the wicked,
for the LORD will be at your side
   and will keep your foot from being snared.

(Proverbs 3:25-26)

Fear of man will prove to be a snare,
but whoever trusts in the LORD is kept safe.
(Proverbs 29:25)

"Peace I leave with you; my peace I give you. I do not give to you as the world gives. Do not let your hearts be troubled and do not be afraid" *(John 14:27)*.

"I have told you these things, so that in me you may have peace. In this world you will have trouble. But take heart! I have overcome the world" *(John 16:33)*.

And we know that in all things God works for the good of those who love him, who have been called according to his purpose *(Romans 8:28)*.

So we say with confidence, "The Lord is my helper; I will not be afraid. What can mere mortals do to me?" *(Hebrews 13:6)*.

Perfect love drives out fear *(1 John 4:18)*.

Dear God, next time I'm afraid help me remember this verse:

_____

_____

_____

Verses for When **You're Lonely**

By day the LORD directs his love,
    at night his song is with me—
    a prayer to the God of my life.

(Psalm 42:8)

He heals the brokenhearted
    and binds up their wounds.

(Psalm 147:3)

"Can a mother forget the baby at her breast
    and have no compassion on the child she has
        borne?
Though she may forget,
    I will not forget you!
See, I have engraved you on the palms of my
        hands;
    your walls are ever before me."

(Isaiah 49:15-16)

"Surely I am with you always, to the very end of
the age" (Matthew 28:20).

For I am convinced that neither death nor life,
neither angels nor demons, neither the present
nor the future, nor any powers, neither height
nor depth, nor anything else in all creation, will

be able to separate us from the love of God that is in Christ Jesus our Lord *(Romans 8:38-39)*.

Lord, next time I'm lonely I'm going to remember this verse:

_____

_____

_____

Verses for When **You Feel Sad**

Why, my soul, are you downcast?
    Why so disturbed within me?
Put your hope in God,
    for I will yet praise him,
    my Savior and my God.

(Psalm 43:5)

"Call on me in the day of trouble;
    I will deliver you, and you will honor me."

(Psalm 50:15)

Cast your cares on the LORD
    and he will sustain you;
he will never let
    the righteous be shaken.

(Psalm 55:22)

Those who hope in the LORD
    will renew their strength.
They will soar on wings like eagles;
    they will run and not grow weary,
    they will walk and not be faint.

(Isaiah 40:31)

"Do not fear, for I am with you;
    do not be dismayed, for I am your God.
I will strengthen you and help you;
    I will uphold you with my righteous right
        hand."

(Isaiah 41:10)

I called on your name, LORD,
    from the depths of the pit.
You heard my plea: "Do not close your ears
    to my cry for relief."
You came near when I called you,
    and you said, "Do not fear."

(Lamentations 3:55-57)

Jesus, I know You care about me when I'm sad because Your Word says so in this verse:

_____

_____

_____

Verses for When **You Need Comfort**

The LORD is a refuge for the oppressed,
> a stronghold in times of trouble.
>> *(Psalm 9:9)*

The LORD is my rock, my fortress and my
> deliverer;
> my God is my rock, in whom I take refuge,
> my shield and the horn of my salvation, my
> stronghold.
>> *(Psalm 18:2)*

For his anger lasts only a moment,
> but his favor lasts a lifetime;
weeping may stay for the night,
> but rejoicing comes in the morning.
>> *(Psalm 30:5)*

The LORD is close to the brokenhearted
> and saves those who are crushed in spirit.
>> *(Psalm 34:18)*

God is our refuge and strength,
> an ever-present help in trouble.
Therefore we will not fear, though the earth give way
> and the mountains fall into the heart of the sea.
>> *(Psalm 46:1-2)*

Though you have made me see troubles,
  many and bitter,
  you will restore my life again;
from the depths of the earth
  you will again bring me up.
You will increase my honor
  and comfort me once more.

(Psalm 71:20-21)

The LORD is good,
  a refuge in times of trouble.
He cares for those who trust in him.

(Nahum 1:7)

Praise be to the God and Father of our Lord Jesus Christ, the Father of compassion and the God of all comfort, who comforts us in all our troubles, so that we can comfort those in any trouble with the comfort we ourselves receive from God *(2 Corinthians 1:3-4).*

Dear God, when I need to feel Your comfort I'll remember this verse:

_____

_____

_____

Verses for When **You Are Tempted to Do the Wrong Thing**

Blessed is the one
     who does not walk in step with the wicked
or stand in the way that sinners take
     or sit in the company of mockers,
but whose delight is in the law of the LORD,
     and who meditates on his law day and night.
                                        (Psalm 1:1)

My son, if sinful men entice you,
     do not give in to them.
                                        (Proverbs 1:10)

Do not set foot on the path of the wicked
     or walk in the way of evildoers.
Avoid it, do not travel on it;
     turn from it and go on your way.
                                        (Proverbs 4:14-15)

Walk with the wise and become wise,
     for a companion of fools suffers harm.
                                        (Proverbs 13:20)

Do not conform to the pattern of this world, but
be transformed by the renewing of your mind
(Romans 12:2).

No temptation has overtaken you except what is common to mankind. And God is faithful; he will not let you be tempted beyond what you can bear. But when you are tempted, he will provide a way out so that you can endure it *(1 Corinthians 10:13).*

Do not be misled: "Bad company corrupts good character" *(1 Corinthians 15:33).*

Am I now trying to win the approval of human beings, or of God? *(Galatians 1:10).*

Because he himself suffered when he was tempted, he is able to help those who are being tempted *(Hebrews 2:18).*

Jesus, next time I'm tempted to sin I'll remember what You said in Your Word:

_____

_____

_____

Verses for When **You've Done Something Wrong**

Blessed is the one
   whose transgressions are forgiven,
   whose sins are covered.
Blessed is the one
   whose sin the LORD does not count against
     them
   and in whose spirit is no deceit...
Then I acknowledged my sin to you
   and did not cover up my iniquity.
I said, "I will confess
   my transgressions to the LORD."
And you forgave the guilt of my sin.
(Psalm 32:1-2,5)

As far as the east is from the west,
   so far has he removed our transgressions
     from us.
(Psalm 103:12)

If you, LORD, kept a record of sins,
   Lord, who could stand?
But with you there is forgiveness,
   so that we can, with reverence, serve you.
(Psalm 130:3-4)

"I, even I, am he who blots out
   your transgressions, for my own sake,
   and remembers your sins no more."
                              (Isaiah 43:25)

There is now no condemnation for those who are in Christ Jesus *(Romans 8:1)*.

If anyone is in Christ, the new creation has come: The old has gone, the new is here! *(2 Corinthians 5:17)*.

In him we have redemption through his blood, the forgiveness of sins, in accordance with the riches of God's grace that he lavished on us *(Ephesians 1:7-8)*.

When you were dead in your sins...God made you alive with Christ. He forgave us all our sins, having canceled the charge of our legal indebtedness, which stood against us and condemned us; he has taken it away, nailing it to the cross *(Colossians 2:13-14)*.

"I will forgive their wickedness and will remember their sins no more" *(Hebrews 8:12)*.

If we confess our sins, he is faithful and just and will forgive us our sins and purify us from all unrighteousness *(1 John 1:9)*.

Lord, I know I've sinned, and I'm so grateful for the forgiveness You promised in this verse:

_____

_____

_____

Verses for When **You're Stressed and Worried**

You will keep in perfect peace
    those whose minds are steadfast,
    because they trust in you.
Trust in the LORD forever,
    for the LORD, the LORD himself, is the Rock
      eternal.

                             (Isaiah 26:3-4)

"Come to me, all you who are weary and burdened, and I will give you rest. Take my yoke upon you and learn from me, for I am gentle and humble in heart, and you will find rest for your souls. For my yoke is easy and my burden is light" *(Matthew 11:28-30)*.

"Peace I leave with you; my peace I give you. I do not give to you as the world gives. Do not let your hearts be troubled and do not be afraid" *(John 14:27)*.

And we know that in all things God works for the good of those who love him, who have been called according to his purpose *(Romans 8:28)*.

Do not be anxious about anything, but in every situation, by prayer and petition, with thanksgiving, present your requests to God. And the peace of God, which transcends all understanding, will guard your hearts and your minds in Christ Jesus *(Philippians 4:6-7)*.

My God will meet all your needs according to the riches of his glory in Christ Jesus *(Philippians 4:19)*.

Jesus, next time I get worried about the future I'll remember what You told me in this verse:

_____

_____

_____

Letting God's Word Change Your Life

1. Make Bible-reading a habit. Try to read a little every day.

2. Don't settle for a surface understanding of God's Word. Study and learn and grow.

3. Reading the Bible is a lifelong journey. Read it all. Read it again!

4. Pray passages of the Bible into your life. Read with God at your side and prayer on your lips.

5. Study with friends. They'll see things you might have missed.

6. Let the Bible do its work on you, transforming your mind, your heart, your emotions, and your spirit.